FUELING SUCCESS : POWER OF

NETWORKING IN BUSINESS

Dr. A. K.Saxena, Ph.D., M.B.A.,LL.B.

TABLE OF CONTENTS

2. Importance of Networking and how it can help grow business

3. The Art of building relationship in business

4. Why relationships matter in business

5. Strategies for building strong relationships in business

6. The importance of relationships in business growth

7. Some Famous Quotes about building strong relationships

8. The importance of communication in building relationships

   as part of networking for business

9. Identifying networking opportunities and how you can make most of them

10. Identifying your networking goals: and how to make most out of these

INTRODUCTION

In today's competitive and ever-changing business landscape, networking has become an essential tool for success. It is not only about exchanging business cards or attending networking events but also about building lasting relationships that can help businesses grow. By building an extensive network of people, businesses can expand their reach, tap into new markets, and generate new opportunities. Networking also provides a platform to exchange ideas, feedback, and recommendations with trusted colleagues, mentors, and peers, which can lead to fresh perspectives and innovative solutions to business problems.

Networking often is one of the most challenging aspects of business, but it can be the most rewarding as it can lead to significant benefits. This book "Networking for Better Outreach and Relations in Business" will be your guide to developing a strong, professional network. It will teach you how to identify networking opportunities, how to master the art of making introductions, how to develop meaningful relationships, and how to leverage your network to achieve your objectives. It will also explore how effective communication, online networking, and handling rejection play a crucial role in building successful networks.

Whether you are just starting out in your business or are looking to build your existing network further, "Networking for Better Outreach and Relations in Business" will provide you with the tools and strategies you need to thrive in today's business environment. So, pick up this book, unleash the power of networking, and take your business to the next level!

2. IMPORTANCE OF NETWORKING AND HOW IT CAN HELP GROW BUSINESS

Networking refers to the process of building relationships with other professionals in your industry or related industries. These relationships can help you expand your reach, build your reputation, and learn from others in your field.

One of the main benefits of networking is that it can help you build your customer base. When you network with other professionals and business owners, you have the opportunity to learn about their products and services. You can then refer your own clients to them, and they can do the same for you. This can help you build a strong referral network that will help you attract new customers and generate more business.

Networking can also help you build your reputation as an authority in your field. When you attend industry events and participate in online communities, you have the opportunity to share your own expertise and offer guidance to others. This can help you establish yourself as a leader in your industry, which can help attract new clients and opportunities.

Furthermore, networking can help you learn about new trends and best practices in your field. When you attend industry events or participate in online groups, you have the opportunity to learn from others and stay up-to-date on the latest developments in your industry. This knowledge can help you make informed decisions about your own business and stay ahead of the competition.

In conclusion, networking is an important tool for businesses looking to grow and expand. By building relationships with other professionals and business owners, you can expand your reach, build your reputation, and stay up-to-date on the latest trends and best practices in your field. So, don't hesitate to get out there and start networking today!

3. THE ART OF BUILDING RELATIONSHOPS IN BUSINESS

In today's competitive business world, it's not just what you know, but who you know that often makes the difference between success and failure. Building strong relationships with your colleagues, clients, and partners is crucial to achieving your goals and making progress in your career. However, building these relationships can be an art form in itself. In this article, we will explore the art of building relationships in business, including strategies, tips, and techniques to help you build strong, lasting relationships.

The growth of any business hinges on its ability to build and maintain strong relationships with its customers, employees, partners, suppliers, and stakeholders. In today's fast-paced, hyper-connected business world, this can be a daunting task. However, successful entrepreneurs and industrialists have long recognized the strategic importance of nurturing strong relationships at all levels of the organization, and investing time and resources to build long-lasting bonds of trust, loyalty, and mutual respect. In this article, we will take a closer look at the art of building relationships for the growth of business, and draw inspiration from some of the most successful and respected businessmen and industrialists of our time.

In today's competitive business world, it's not just what you know, but who you know that often makes the difference between success and failure. Building strong relationships with your colleagues, clients, and partners is crucial to achieving your goals and making progress in your career. However, building these relationships can be an art form in itself. In this article, we will explore the art of building relationships in business, including strategies, tips, and techniques to help you build strong, lasting relationships.

Why Relationships Matter in Business

The importance of building relationships in business cannot be overstated. Whether you are seeking to build your client base, advance your career, or grow your business, strong relationships can help you achieve your goals. Here are some reasons why relationships matter in business:

- *Improved communication*: Building strong relationships improves communication and understanding between you and your clients or colleagues. This can help you work more effectively together and achieve better results.

- *Increased trust*: Strong relationships are built on trust. By cultivating trust, you create a foundation for long-term partnerships that can benefit both parties in the long run.

- *Opportunities for collaboration*: Strong relationships can also lead to opportunities for collaboration, allowing you to leverage each other's strengths and work together towards common goals.

- *Increased loyalty*: When clients feel that they have a strong relationship with you and your business, they are more likely to remain loyal and recommend your products or services to others.

Strategies for Building Strong Relationships

Building strong relationships in business takes time, effort, and patience. Here are some strategies that can help you build relationships that last:

1. *Be authentic.* Authenticity is key in building strong relationships. Be yourself, show an interest in others, and stay true to your values. This will help build a genuine rapport with others.

2. *Listen actively:* Active listening is a critical component of building strong relationships. Pay attention to what others are saying, and show genuine interest in their thoughts and opinions.

3. *Build reciprocal relationships.* A strong relationship is built on give and take. By offering your expertise and support to others, you create opportunities for them to do the same for you.

4. ***Be timely and responsive***: In today's fast-paced business environment, time is of the essence. Be timely and responsive in your communications, and follow up on commitments and promises.

5. ***Attend networking events***: Networking events provide excellent opportunities to meet new people and build relationships. Attend events where you can connect with others in your industry or community.

6. ***Use social media strategically***: Social media has become an essential tool for building relationships in business. Use social media to stay connected with others, share relevant content, and engage in conversations.

7. *Remember the little things.* Small gestures can make a big difference in building strong relationships. Remember the little things, such as birthdays, anniversaries, and other milestones.

---

4. WHY RELATIONSHIPS MATTER IN BUSINESS

The importance of building relationships in business cannot be overstated. Whether you are seeking to build your client base, advance your career, or grow your business, strong relationships can help you achieve your goals. Here are some reasons why relationships matter in business:

- *Improved communication:* Building strong relationships improves communication and understanding between you and your clients or colleagues. This can help you work more effectively together and achieve better results.

- *Increased trust:* Strong relationships are built on trust. By cultivating trust, you create a foundation for long-term partnerships that can benefit both parties in the long run.

- *Opportunities for collaboration:* Strong relationships can also lead to opportunities for collaboration, allowing you to leverage each other's strengths and work together towards common goals.

- *Increased loyalty:* When clients feel that they have a strong relationship with you and your business, they are more likely to remain loyal and recommend your products or services to others.

5. STRATEGIES FOR BUILDING STRONG RELATIONSHIPS

Building strong relationships in business takes time, effort, and patience. Here are some strategies that can help you build relationships that last:

1. *Be authentic:* Authenticity is key in building strong relationships. Be yourself, show an interest in others, and stay true to your values. This will help build a genuine rapport with others.

2. *Listen actively:* Active listening is a critical component of building strong relationships. Pay attention to what others are saying, and show genuine interest in their thoughts and opinions.

3. *Build reciprocal relationships:* A strong relationship is built on give and take. By offering your expertise and support to others, you create opportunities for them to do the same for you.

4. *Be timely and responsive*: In today's fast-paced business environment, time is of the essence. Be timely and responsive in your communications, and follow up on commitments and promises.

5. *Attend networking events*: Networking events provide excellent opportunities to meet new people and build relationships. Attend events where you can connect with others in your industry or community.

6. *Use social media strategically*: Social media has become an essential tool for building relationships in business. Use social media to stay connected with others, share relevant content, and engage in conversations.

7. *Remember the little things.* Small gestures can make a big difference in building strong relationships. Remember the little things, such as birthdays, anniversaries, and other milestones.

8. *Build a strong network.* Successful businessmen and industrialists recognize the importance of building a strong network of trusted contacts, including customers, employees, partners, suppliers, and stakeholders. They attend networking events, participate in industry associations, and use social media strategically to build and expand their network.

9. *Communicate effectively.* Successful businessmen and industrialists know that effective communication is key to building strong relationships. They are clear, concise, and persuasive in their communications, and they adapt their style to the needs of their audience.

10. *Demonstrate expertise and value.* Successful businessmen and industrialists understand that building strong relationships requires demonstrating expertise and value to their customers, employees, partners, and suppliers. They share knowledge, provide guidance, and offer innovative solutions to their stakeholders' challenges, needs, and aspirations.

11. *Be responsive and dependable.* Successful businessmen and industrialists know that building trust with their stakeholders requires being responsive and dependable. They respond quickly to requests and inquiries, follow through on commitments, and show a genuine, sustained interest in the well-being and success of their stakeholders.

12. *Invest in life-long learning.* Successful businessmen and industrialists are committed to life-long learning, and they invest time, energy, and resources to keep up-to-date on the latest trends, technologies, and best practices in their industry. They continuously seek out new ideas, insights, and perspectives that can help them grow and improve their business, and they share their knowledge and

expertise generously with their stakeholders.

---

6. THE IMPORTANCE OF RELATINSHIPS IN BUSINESS GROWTH

Relationships are the foundation of business growth. By building strong, meaningful relationships with their stakeholders, businesses can achieve a range of strategic benefits, including:

- *Enhanced customer satisfaction and loyalty.* By building trust and rapport with customers, businesses can create a loyal customer base that is more likely to return for repeat business and recommend the company to others.

- *Improved employee engagement and retention*: By fostering a culture of trust and respect, businesses can attract, retain, and engage talented and committed employees, who can contribute to the company's growth and success over the long term.

- *Better supplier and partner relationships*: By nurturing strong relationships with suppliers and partners, businesses can gain access to new markets, products, and services, and share knowledge and expertise to achieve mutual growth and success.

- *Enhanced reputation and brand equity*: By building a reputation as a trusted, reliable, and responsible business partner, companies can enhance their brand equity, attract new customers and investors, and boost their revenue and profitability.

---

7. FAMOUS QUOTES ON RELATIONSHIP BUILDING FOR BUSINESS GROWTH

Here are some famous quotes that can inspire you in building strong relationships for the growth of business:

- *"Business is all about relationships...how well you build them determines how well they build your business. "*- Brad Sugars

- *"Start by doing what's necessary; then do what's possible, and suddenly you are doing the impossible."* - Francis of Assisi

- *"The biggest barrier to growth is often ourselves. We have to overcome our fears and comfort zones and take calculated risks to move forward."* - Richard Branson

- *"The success of your business depends on the mentorship, sponsorship, and partnership of others."* - Michael Hyatt

- "*A business that makes nothing but money is a poor business.*" - Henry Ford

- "The currency of real networking is not greed but generosity." - Keith Ferrazzi

- "The most important single ingredient in the formula of success is knowing how to get along with people." - Theodore Roosevelt

- "People do business with people they know, like, and trust." - Bob Burg

- "*It takes 20 years to build a reputation and five minutes to ruin it. If you think about that, you'll do things differently.*" - Warren Buffett

8. THE IMPORTANCE OF COMMUNICATION IN BUILDING RELATIONSHIPS AS PART OF NETWORKING FOR BUSINESS

Effective communication is essential for building relationships and growing your business. When you effectively communicate your ideas, needs, and goals with others, you establish trust, build rapport, and create stronger connections.

One of the main benefits of effective communication in building relationships is the ability to build trust. When you communicate openly and honestly with others, you demonstrate your integrity and reliability. This builds trust and makes others more likely to work with you and refer business to you.

Effective communication also helps you build rapport and connect with others on a deeper level. When you take the time to listen to others and understand their needs and concerns, you show that you are genuinely interested in building a relationship. This can help you create strong connections and build a network of professional contacts that can support your business growth.

Furthermore, effective communication is essential for resolving conflicts and negotiating deals. When you are able to articulate your position clearly and listen to the other person's perspective, you can find common ground and work towards a mutually beneficial solution. This can help you maintain positive relationships and avoid damaging conflicts that can harm your business.

Another benefit of effective communication is that it can help you build your reputation as a skilled communicator. When you are known as a good listener and a clear communicator, others will be more likely to seek out your expertise and refer business to you. This can help you establish yourself as a leader in your industry and attract new opportunities and clients.

In conclusion, effective communication is a critical component of building relationships as part of networking for business. By building trust, connecting with others on a deeper level, resolving conflicts, and building your reputation as a skilled communicator, you can establish a strong network of professional contacts that can support your business growth and help you achieve your goals. So, focus on improving your communication skills and building strong relationships, and watch your business thrive!

9. IDENTIFYING NETWORKING OPPORTUNITIES AND HOW

YOU CAN MAKE MOST OF THEM

Networking is an essential tool for professionals looking to advance their careers or establish new business ventures. Successful networking requires identifying opportunities and leveraging them to create meaningful connections that can provide support and further professional development. In this article, we will explore some ways to identify networking opportunities and make the most of them.

1. *Attend Industry Events and Conferences*

Attending industry events and conferences provides an excellent opportunity to meet peers and leaders in your field. These events offer an environment where people from different organizations come together to share ideas and information. By attending these events, you can stay up-to-date on the trends and practices in your field and expand your knowledge while also making valuable connections.

2. *Join Professional Associations or Organizations*

Joining an association or organization affiliated with your profession is another great way to make connections. These groups offer opportunities to learn and grow through events, workshops, training sessions, and mentorships. You can also connect with others in your field, share ideas, and even find job openings.

3. *Attend Local Meet-ups or Community Events*

Local meetups or community events offer a less formal, more social setting for professionals to connect. They are often more relaxed and provide a chance to meet new people and build relationships with those in your local area. Look for opportunities to participate in events that interest you, such as fundraisers, charity events, or hobby groups.

4. *Use Social Media and Other Online Platforms*

Social media provides an immediate and effective means to connect with others in your field. By following industry experts, joining groups or forums, and engaging with others online, you can build relationships with other professionals in your field. LinkedIn is a popular platform for professionals looking to expand their networks, but other social media platforms such as Twitter and Facebook can also be effective tools.

5. *Attend Career or Job Fairs*

Career or job fairs provide an excellent opportunity to meet and connect with employers and recruiters in your field. They offer an easy way to network with multiple organizations in one location. You can learn about potential job opportunities and get valuable advice on your career path.

<u>Once you identify networking opportunities, it is important to remember some key tips to leverage them effectively:</u>

1. *Be Authentic.* Authenticity in networking is crucial. Engage in conversations that are meaningful and show genuine interest in others. Avoid trying to sell yourself or your products at networking events.

2. *Be Prepared.* Before attending any networking event, research those who will be in attendance and prepare for any eventuality. Review their profiles and research their organizations so you can ask informed questions, add comments, or pick up on interesting topics they ha vet outlined.

3. *Follow Up.* The most successful networking comes from strong follow-up.

After attending a conference or event, remember to follow up with new contacts so you can keep the conversation moving forward. This is usually best achieved via email or social media.

4. *Create a good impression*: Dress professionally, exude confidence, be polite, and display good etiquette. Try to get to know the person you are speaking with, listen carefully, and remember their name. This will help you make a positive and lasting impression.

Final Thoughts

Networking is an important part of professional development. By identifying networking opportunities, attending events, and making meaningful connections, you can open up doors to new career opportunities, potential partnerships, and collaborations. Remember, networking is all about building relationships over time, and not a one-time deal. With persistence and consistency, your networking efforts will yield successful results.

10. HOW TO IDENTIFY YOUR NETWORKING GOALS TO MAKE THE MOST OUT OF NETWORKING

Networking is all about building meaningful and authentic relationships with others. Creating strong connections can be a key driver in your career success;

however, it's not just about meeting as many people as possible. When networking, it's important to have clear goals in mind to make sure that your efforts are focused and effective.

1. *Define Your Purpose*

The first step in identifying your networking goals is to define your purpose. Determine what you want to achieve from networking. Are you looking to increase your knowledge, expand your professional circle, or find new career opportunities? Knowing your purpose will give you a clear direction when it comes to finding and attending networking events.

2. *Assess Your Current Professional Network*

Before you start attending networking events, take an assessment of your current network, and identify gaps in that network. Determine the people who are missing from your network and what types of connections would be beneficial. Think about what types of professionals are relevant to your current or desired career path and what specific expertise you may need.

3. *Focus on Building Relationships*

Once you have identified the people and expertise that you need to add to your network, focus on building relationships with them. Networking is not a one-time deal; it requires ongoing effort and maintenance. Build relationships with professionals in the fields you're interested in; these relationships will yield long-term benefits, such as advice when you need it.

4. *Attend Relevant Networking Events*

When it comes to attending networking events, it's about quality, not quantity. When identifying your networking goals, consider which types of events are most relevant to you and your industry. Being strategic with your time by attending relevant events will give you the most opportunities to connect with professionals who will help you further your career.

5. *Track Your Progress*

It's important to track your progress toward your networking goals. Keep a log of the people you meet, what you learned from them, and their contact information. Follow up with your contacts within 24-48 hours of meeting them to keep the connection strong. You can also set networking goals for yourself and track them, which will help motivate you and determine your effectiveness.

6. *Participate in Online Networking*

Networking isn't just about face-to-face interactions at events; it can also be achieved online. Participate in LinkedIn and other social media platforms to connect and engage with other professionals. Taking part in relevant forums and groups can help you build connections with a network of individuals who share your interests and goals.

Final Thoughts

Networking is an essential part of building a successful career. Identifying your networking goals will give you a clear direction on the types of events to attend, the people to meet, and the conversations to have. Be strategic with your networking efforts, keep track of your progress, and focus on building authentic relationships with professionals who can help further your career. Above all, stay positive, be genuine, and don't be afraid to step out of your comfort zone. With time and effort, you'll find that building a strong network is one of the best investments you can make in your professional life.

11. HOW TO MAKE EFFECTIVE INTRODUCIONS THAT CAN

HELP CREATE LASTING CONNECTIONS FOR BUSINESS

In business, making effective introductions can make all the difference in building lasting relationships with potential clients, partners, and collaborators. However, introducing people to each other can be tricky if you're not sure how to do it properly. In this article, we will explore some tips on how to make effective introductions that help create lasting connections for business.

1. *Know the People you're Introducing*

One of the first and most important steps to making effective introductions is to know the people you're introducing. Research them beforehand or get to know them personally so that you can introduce them accurately and confidently. You should also make sure to get their permission before introducing them to others.

2. *Start with the Common Ground*

When making introductions, it's a good idea to start with the common ground that the two people share. This will help to create a positive connection and start a more meaningful conversation. For instance, you can mention a mutual interest, project, or industry experience that you know both parties have in common.

3. *Use Their Names and Titles*

When introducing people, always use their full names and titles. This shows respect and professionalism. Make sure you provide the correct pronunciation of their names and preferable spellings. Also, provide an overview of their titles and roles so that others have a clear understanding of their expertise or place in the industry.

4. *Provide Context*

Be sure to provide context for the introductions, as this will help people understand why you're introducing them and what they can expect from each other. You can mention a problem you think they could help each other solve or present a shared goal. This will provide initial insights which the parties can use to start conversing.

5. *Follow up After the Introduction*

After you've made the introduction, follow up with both parties to see how things went. Once you have introduced them, communication is key. Have a short chat with each of them to check on how they connected with their new partner. Additionally, this creates an accountability loop ensuring that the connection doesn't die prematurely.

6. *Foster a Comfortable Environment*

Finally, it is important to foster a comfortable environment during the introduction. Attend to the body language of all people involved. Gauge the comfort level of each person and ensure the atmosphere during the introduction is not intimidating.

Final Thoughts

In conclusion, making effective introductions is a vital aspect of the business world when it comes to building lasting connections. Be well-prepared and create a positive introduction experience that focuses on the common ground. Be aware of the context and the parties involved, follow up with each one, and provide a comfortable environment. These simple tips will help you create introductions that will lead to strong connections and long-lasting relationships that are good for your business.

---

12. BUILDING MEANINGFUL RELATIONSHIPS AND TIPS ON HOW TO NURTURE AND DEVELOP POSITIVE RELATIONSHIPS WITH YOUR NETWORK

In today's fast-paced, tech-driven world, networking and building relationships with people in your professional and personal lives are more important than ever.

However, it's not just about meeting new people but also nurturing and building meaningful relationships that are long-lasting and impactful. In this article, we will explore some tips on how to develop and maintain positive relationships with people in your network.

1. *Show Genuine Interest*

The most crucial aspect of building a meaningful relationship is to show genuine interest in the person's life and work. Take the initiative to attend events and meetings where you can develop your relationship with them. During conversations, listen actively, and show empathy. This will help you better understand their perspective and build stronger connections.

2. *Be Authentic*

Authenticity is key when building relationships. Stay true to who you are and be open and transparent in your conversations. Avoid trying to be someone you're not, or pretending to be interested in something you're not passionate about. This will help you create a more meaningful, long-term connection that is based on trust.

3. *Stay in Touch*

The best way to maintain a successful relationship is to stay in touch regularly. This means keeping in contact on a regular basis, whether it's through phone calls, emails, social media, or in-person meetings. Make a habit of checking in with your contacts from time to time to remain engaged.

4. *Provide Value*

If you want to continue to build and strengthen your relationships, it's essential to provide value to your contacts. Look for ways to support them, whether it's by offering your expertise or building a bridge to connect them to someone who can help with their career or projects. Providing value is a critical component of maintaining long-term relationships.

5. *Be Consistent*

Consistency is essential for building positive relationships. This means catching up with contacts and providing value on a regular basis. It also means keeping your commitments and being reliable. Even small gestures such as sending a message on holidays or special occasions can help to keep your relationships fresh.

6. *Take Initiative*

Finally, be proactive about developing your relationships. Make the first move to reach out, schedule meetings, and initiate conversations. Don't always wait for the other person to make the first move. Taking the initiative will demonstrate your interest in the relationship and show that it's important to you.

Final Thoughts

Building meaningful relationships takes time, effort, and intentionality. By taking the time to listen actively, showing genuine interest, staying in touch regularly, providing value, being consistent, and taking initiative, you can create stronger and deeper connections with your contacts. These qualities will help you build a strong and supportive network of friends, colleagues, and mentors who can help you achieve your personal and professional goals. Remember to approach every interaction with authenticity and the desire to learn and grow together, and you will be well on your way to nurturing meaningful relationships.

---

13. HOW TO HANDLE REJECTION AND OVERCOME OBSTACLES IN NETWORKING

In life, we all face rejection or obstacles at some point. However, knowing how to handle rejection and overcome obstacles is critical in networking. Here we will share some strategies on how to deal with rejection and overcome obstacles when networking.

1. *Reframe rejection*: When you face rejection, it can be tempting to view it as a personal failure. However, it is important to reframe rejection by understanding that it is a natural part of the networking process. Instead of seeing it as a failure, view rejection as an opportunity to learn and improve your networking skills.

2. *Keep a positive mind-set*: When facing obstacles or rejection, keeping a positive mind-set is essential. This can help you remain focused on your goals and keep you motivated. Remember that every obstacle or rejection can be an opportunity to learn or grow.

3. *Evaluate the situation*: When facing rejection or obstacles, take time to evaluate

the situation. Identify any areas where you can improve and make adjustments accordingly. Doing this can help you to approach similar situations differently in the future.

4. *Seek feedback:* Seek feedback from your connections or other professionals in your industry. Be open to constructive criticism and use that feedback to make improvements.

5. *Use rejection as a motivator.* Instead of letting rejection discourage you, use it as a motivator to work even harder. Keep networking and get involved in different events to expand your network.

6. *Have a strong support system*: Having a strong support system can be crucial when facing rejection or obstacles. Family, friends, and mentors can provide emotional support, advice, and insights from their experiences.

In conclusion, handling rejection and overcoming obstacles is a necessary part of the networking process. Reframing rejection, keeping a positive mind-set, evaluating the situation, seeking feedback, using rejection as a motivator, and having a support system can all help in dealing with rejection and overcoming obstacles when networking. Remember, networking is a process, and with the right strategies and persistence, you can achieve your networking goals.

14. NETWORKING DURING DIGITAL ERA

In today's digital age, networking has gone online. With social media and other online platforms, it has become easier to connect with people in various industries, build relationships, and grow your professional network. In this article, we will share some tips on how you can use social media and other online platforms to effectively network and build meaningful connections.

1. *Choose the right platforms*: Not all social media platforms are created equal, and each platform attracts different types of

professionals. Identify which platforms your target audience is most likely to be on, and focus your efforts on those platforms.

2. *Optimize your profile:* Your online profiles are often the first impression that you make on potential connections. Optimize your profile by including a professional photo, a clear and concise bio, and highlighting your skills and accomplishments.

3. *Share valuable content:* Share valuable content that your network would be interested in, such as industry-related news, articles or blog posts. This helps to establish you as a thought leader in your field and keeps your network engaged with you.

4. *Engage in conversations*: Engage in conversations with your connections by commenting on their posts or starting your own threads. This helps to build relationships and establish you as an active and valuable member of your network.

5. *Participate in relevant groups*: Join groups that are relevant to your industry or professional interests. Participate in discussions, offer your insights and knowledge, and add value to the group. This helps to expand your network and build new connections.

6. *Initiate conversations*: Don't be afraid to initiate conversations with potential connections. Send those personalized

messages or emails, and offer value or insight that could be helpful to them.

7. *Attend virtual events*: Attend virtual events such as webinars or conferences related to your industry or profession. This provides a great opportunity to meet new people, learn about the latest industry trends, and expand your network.

In conclusion, online networking has become an essential part of networking in today's digital age. By choosing the right platforms, optimizing your profiles, sharing valuable content, engaging in conversations, participating in relevant groups, initiating conversations, and attending virtual events, you can effectively network and build meaningful connections that can help you to achieve your career goals.

---

15. EPILOGUE

In today's world, building successful networks has become more important than ever. Having a strong network can help you in many ways, from finding a new job to forming new partnerships with other businesses. However, to build an effective network, you need to know how to leverage those connections and use them to achieve your objectives. In this article, we will share some strategies on how to do this effectively.

1. *Keep in touch*: It is important to keep in touch with your connections, even if you do not need their help. Establish an on-going communication channel with them, ask them how they are doing, and offer them any support they may need. Doing this will help you build a stronger relationship with your connections.

2. *be specific with your requests*: When you need help, be specific with your requests. Make sure to clearly outline what you want, why you want it, and how it can benefit your connection. Doing this will help your connections to better understand your request and they will be able to help you more effectively.

3. *Offer help*: Networking is about building relationships, not just asking for help. Be willing to offer your help to your connections whenever possible. This shows that you value the relationship and are not just looking for something in return.

4. *Attend events*: Attend events that are relevant to your industry or profession. This will help you meet new people and create new connections. Also, make sure to follow up with the people you meet after the event. This is where your on-going communication channel will come in handy.

5. *Show gratitude*: When someone helps you, make sure to show your gratitude. Thank them for their help and let them

know how much you appreciate it. Doing this shows that you value their contributions and helps to strengthen the relationship.

Building effective networks takes time and effort. However, if you keep in touch, be specific with your requests, offer help, attend events and show gratitude, you will be well on your way to building a strong network that can help you achieve your objectives effectively. Networking has become an essential part of business and industry today. Many great businessmen and industrialists have shared their opinions and views on the role and significance of networking in the success of a business.

One of the most well-known advocates of networking is *Sir Richard Branson*, founder of the Virgin Group. Branson said that "□□Succeeding in business is all about making connections."□□ He goes on to suggest that networking is the most important part of building a successful business, as it allows entrepreneurs to meet new people, exchange ideas, and discover new opportunities.

Another successful businessman, *Bill Gates*, emphasized the importance of networking in the digital age. Gates said," *The internet is becoming the town square for the global village of tomorrow. Networking is vital to its success.*" These words are especially relevant today, as social media and other digital platforms have become the primary means of personal and professional communication.

Another great industrialist, *Andrew Carnegie*, believed that networking was essential to achieving success. He believed that *"No man can become rich without himself enriching others."* By networking and creating strong relationships with other professionals, *Carnegie* believed that individuals could improve their own standing in the business world while also helping others.

Lastly, *Oprah Winfrey*, the media executive and philanthropist, acknowledged the importance of networking for personal growth. She once said,"*Surround yourself with only people who are going to lift you higher."*□□ *Oprah* believed that by building a network of supportive individuals, you can achieve your goals and reach new height.

In conclusion, networking has become a vital part of business and industry success. The opinions and views of great businessmen and industrialists indicate that by building strong relationships with others and making connections, one can achieve success in their career and personal life. It is essential to remember that networking is not just about exchanging business cards or making sales, but rather about forming strong connections and creating a supportive community.